My Hometown

Burley Idaho

By

Robert Bailey Lee Carmody

authorHOUSE™

1663 LIBERTY DRIVE, SUITE 200
BLOOMINGTON, INDIANA 47403
(800) 839-8640
WWW.AUTHORHOUSE.COM

First published by AuthorHouse 10/08/04

ISBN: 1-4208-0029-9 (sc)
ISBN: 1-4208-0028-0 (dj)

Printed in the United States of America
Bloomington, Indiana

This book is printed on acid-free paper.

PREFACE

I have been blessed with a very wonderful and uncomplicated childhood. My parents and family members were normal, my schooling was the best, and the people whom I associated with during those years were the best. I had role models and they shaped not only the course that our little farm town was taking but the course that I was also taking.

I have so many memories of growing up and lucky for me my mind still can recall most of them. Perhaps some of my spelling is in error and the names of some of the spouses may be fuzzy. I want the reader to go back with me to those simple times when all seemed so easy. Revisit some of the stores in their grandeur. Now, many are absent and more and more empty rooms with paper covered glass windows are all that remain. Times change and cities change. But not so their soul and heart.

I have tried to include as many names as I can recall in hopes that some will return back in time to recount some of their special memories. I am sure that they do exist. I have touched on some political concerns of mine and hope that they are taken in the light of good humor which I intended. For the new people, I hope that they can return to the early days and appreciate more and more of our little town.

Some folks will be left out and yet in my heart and mind they are still there.

The literary style, if there is any, is bouncy but that is the way my mind works.

Pulitzer can't be right all of the time. (Oh my, was there a Pulitzer living in Burley that I forgot?)

I have purposely omitted many people who might be nearer my age and generation. These people count but I wanted to speak to those early days in

Burley Idaho

population then 6000-8000

Birthing

The year was 1937 and a major war was in the developing stages. Naturally I knew nothing about the problems that our country was facing and in fact the entire globe itself was on the brink of major destruction and conquests. I don't recall my mother nor my grandparents discussing the war but of course I was somewhat below the age of any sort of reason and understanding. As my dad was absent at the time in our lives, my prime role model was done magnificently by my dear mother Rita along with 'Nanny" and "Papa" Pence. We all lived on Miller Avenue just across from the Romney Apartments. I never did find out the origin of "Romney" and to this day would welcome an answer. The house was a good house even though the basement was something out of a Hollywood mystery movie. One of my fondest memories were of the coal burning heater and 'clinkers'. Even today I take great fun in challenging my friends and acquaintances on the meaning of 'clinkers'. One would just have to live around coal to appreciate coal buckets and 'clinkers'.

Many great memories of chicken plucking and I do remember them so well with Papa Pence bringing a gunny sack to our home with fresh chickens doing the chicken last dance inside a gunny sack. Out would come the handy dandy single bladed axe and a previously bloodied board which would do the honors. In those times we didn't have the pleasure of dropping over to the local super market and selecting an already cut, skinned, boned, and plastic wrapped morsel for dinner. The unlucky birds were pulled out of the bag one at a time and placed neck down on the sacrificial board and whamo, the bird would exit the scene running around like a 'chicken with his head off'. It was not a pleasant site but somehow the experience didn't turn me into some kind of psyco maniac. So much for those good ole days ladies. But that was what we did.

We didn't have home freezers in those days and I remember the trips to the local freezer boxes owned by Mr. Thornton located next to the Burley Elks club. As various vegetables were prepared and packaged along with occasional meat items, we would venture into that most scary scene and push the mysterious plunger door opening. Entering the insides was a surreal experience and the cold was awful. But most of all was the continuous fear that I might be trapped inside with no way to open that door. Some of my favorite 'butchered' items had to be the salt pork bacon and that home made sausage. At that time high cholesterol and triglycerides hadn't been invented.

Family dinners had to be the highlight in my book of memories. As with most people, we did have many relatives that lived nearby and no excuse was ever needed to gather the clan. The large table with all the leafs in place complete with the crocheted table cloth was barely sufficient to contain all the good things that had been prepared. We all sat around the table in those days with no distractions of television and Play Station One to lure the young set away from the old timers. In fact the thought of leaving this gracious table of events never even entered our minds. Home made ice cream was usually the capping of events and with the ice and salt flowing all over the lawn outside. The first challenge was just who was going to be able to lick the paddles. Then the canister of yummy ice cream was packed with a large rag and ice packed around it until the time of it's ultimate enjoyment. We did have one crisis which never again repeated itself and it involved lemon flavoring in the vanilla ice cream and one of my wonderful aunts. It did create a very momentary show of tears and some awful feelings as to why we didn't omit it in the first place. Needless to say, it was never repeated. This tradition continued up to the later years with my cousin Judy Jolley who initiated the 'happy party' event following late that night after a sumptuous feast. Once more 'damn the calories and full speed ahead!'

Christmas time was always the highlight of the year and all had most lavish family gatherings. For a long time, each person bought gifts for every other person. Of course all this had to be preceded with very delicious meals and fabulous desserts. My two aunts were the queens of desserts with no equal anywhere. Afterwards, the gifts were exchanged and the resultant pile of discarded paper products filled the entire living room. I remember many of those gifts had to have cost a bit and yet we did it. Fortunately, we later faced the facts that costs were going up rapidly and we did resort to the old 'draw names' and impose a' money limit'. That finally ended an era of our little extravagancies.

Bostetter...Even the name brought up mystical memories for me at the time. Papa Pence was the master of our southern Idaho back country mountains. He was the best driver, knew all the mountain men, and loved driving his new Buick over those awful roads. As a family, we made many visits to those south hills for picnics. Fried chicken, baked corn with a magical bread crumb covering, water melon, hot coffee on the outdoor fire, biscuits, homemade relishes, and the family. My dear grandmother Nanny was always the center of the affair and was the real key in putting it together. Often Papa would do the ultimate magic when after sighting a rattlesnake on the road he would stop and quickly dispatch the poor devil with the dropping of large boulders upon his helpless self. So many good times.

Papa was a deer hunter and introduced me to the art and skill of the hunt. I couldn't sleep the night before and we arose early and drove to those south hills. It seemed like ole Bill Bellfield was always the man who would check us to see that we were legal. It was so exciting to enter his darkened tent in the wee hours. Man did Papa know everyone in the world or not!

We drove up to Little Piney and began the hunt. My uncle Hal Jolley and I would take our position on the top of a south facing slope. Then the "spoofing deer thing" commenced with Papa throwing large boulders down the sun exposed brush which was the home of the poor little deer people. Well, they would come flying out only to be met with a hailstorm of bullets all usually missing their marks. Occasionally we would bag a deer and watch as once more Papa displayed his prowess removing all the recognizable parts of the poor deer. Well in time, we would return to the city with our kill and once more chalk up a victory for the hunters of the world. My what a guy!?

Do you remember how they repaired the sewer lines which ran down the alley ways? I was always fascinated with the remains of wooden plugs which were hammered into the leaks. I don't know why they didn't use 'J B Weld' because according to Paul Harvey, it would fix anything..

The War Years

Pearl Harbor was never a memory for me as I was only four years old when the surprise attack put our country into the war. As I recall, we didn't seem to do badly on the home front at our little home. Meals were always good and on time and we didn't seem to want for anything important. I do recall those little square flags with stars in the middle which indicated family in the service and sadly those who has lost family members usually sons and husbands. While working for Morrison-Knudsen on Wake Island, my birth father had been captured and I knew nothing about him. I would learn later that my mom and him had been divorced about that time yet he would continue to write her asking about 'his little boy'. I can still see army trucks parked on the then gravel roads from time to time. For some reason, I had this urge to make a mad dash across the road. Just as I started my mad dashing, John Roper was on his way down the road and hit me (well sort of hit me). I can still see me lying in front of those tires but apparently not too damaged else I would not be writing this, right? Well John must have been a pretty good driver as all went well and as time went on I would be great friends of all the Ropers who lived just through the back alley.

Trips to the Elk's club were always a thrill as I would look on their bulletin board at pictures of our local warriors donned in a variety of aviation gear, naval and army attire. Klink, Church, Manning, and so many more that escape me at the moment. Those were proud picture there and as later years would go by, I would see them often and recall those pictures.

We traveled once to Vallejo California to visit Wanda Jolley where Hal was stationed. I remember those little war stamps found in the ration books,that allowed one to buy only so much of things like sugar, coffee, tires, and those rare items available at the time. Still, I seemed so far away from the war while our men were dying to protect our life here in Burley

I do recall a Prisoner of war camp on the north side which is now all gone and producing farm products. We would go on a couple of occasions to review what remained but it seemed that it made an early vanishing act and most people probably have forgotten that it was ever there. But I remember.

Judge Thomas Bailey Lee

I never really knew this great man. It was simply a subject that was not discussed. It was only after I had made it through the first half of my life that I became interested in the 'roots' things. My earliest recollections of the judge was time spent in their home next to the Terhunes on Burton Avenue. Hooter and I would find it so funny when the judge from out of nowhere would throw these very loud tirades of #$@%&^* as he stomped the floor in some sort of agony. For you see the judge suffered severely with rheumatism and this was his way of dealing with the pain. This man was eloquent and probably could have said the same words in Latin or Greek but of course it wouldn't have been nearly as entertaining. Thomas Bailey Lee Sr was an icon for the Lee history and he traced his roots back almost to God. His ties to the North

Carolina 'Baileys' was perhaps my most shining moment as up until that point I was not too crazy about my middle name of 'Bailey'. You see everywhere I went in the early days I was called 'T Bailey' and I just didn't know. Well after that Bailey was the best and in fact one of my grandsons has been named 'Bailey'. The judge had a great way about him and the law and he eventually went on to the state capitol in Boise and became a Chief Justice of the Idaho Supreme Court . Not to leave his wife Irene (Neeny) out of the picture, she was remembered as always having her famous caramels in the basement drying for later sale as "Mrs.Lee's Inimitables Chocolates".

So all you parents out there don't fail to have your children spend quality time with grandparents and learn the oral tradition of their (and your) own roots. Their grandparents won't be around forever. (And neither will you..) Oh and who was this 'Hooter' person? My sweet cousin and daughter of Mary Scott was 'Irene' and somewhere she was nicknamed "Hooter" or by her mom "Hoot" for short.

Summers

I have traveled to many areas of our great country and must say that nothing, not anything beats our southern Idaho summers. That clean air with a mixture of farm scents of fresh alfalfa and a sprinkle of manure is the best. Those warm summer days with a slight breeze blowing covered by some wispy puffs of cumulus clouds is an artist's mixed green salad delight. And of course at days end, we would sit outside in the back yard and just talk until the wee hours of the final stages of the day. It seem like days would last forever. No smog either. Evenings were spent often with those infamous outside games of 'hide and seek', 'kick the can,' and yes doing slight deeds of mischievous. We were never afraid of being shot, robbed, or molested. I believe that our parents never worried much about what was going on outside.

Alleys which have become a lost idea were our greatest sneak away into the realm of the ultimate sneaky. One could venture anywhere at night with the alleys at our ready.

Bring back the front porches…When the front porch vanished a part of all us vanished. They were the center of our relaxation and especially late in the day as the sun began it's crash into the Pacific. No television to steal our minds but just good 'palaver.' It sure made parents a bit closer to their kid's doings and so also for the kids.

Lilac time was the best and usually there was an abundance of those beautiful and most fragrant of flowers. Oh for one more smell of that glorious aroma. They were usually best observed lining the alleyways. It seemed their moment of glory was achieved on memorial day when the last resting places of our folks were garnished annually. (I never did like those Peonies as they were always covered with little ants.) Would you believe I still find fond times spending a few hours visiting the Pleasant View Cemetery to visit with my old friends.

Then there was a time when many of the ladies on Burton Avenue decided that it would be nice to develop rose gardens along the street at some of the local folks. These sweet people were members of the local bridge club which was affectionately call the "Bon Huer" Club. Anyone speak French? I never saw any men's poker clubs doing the same thing but off course that's not what men's poker games are about, right? Sure enough, many beautiful gardens of fabulous roses sprouted up along the street. Many might be there still although much time as passed and other "stuff' may have displaced them.

"Let there be no fences" was the rule rather than the exception. Play was certainly easy when you had no limits on where you could run or chase people. Neighbors weren't so private then and seldom were we asked to get off of the property. Dogs had a nice run of the place and I suspect that those that were pesky ended up with a well aimed bee-bee gun scare or the old flipper crotch. (And speaking of bee bee guns, they were always supposed to put out your eye. Yet I never met anyone who had their eye "put out".

15

Did You?) I never saw an animal die or even suffer a hurt as a result of these now barbaric cave-man habits.

When was the last time that you purchased asparagus at your local Albertson's? We would load up the faithful car and set out to the country in search of the illusive spear-shaped delicacy. The usual hiding spots were in and around the small and large ditch banks. At the time, they were very plentiful and with a sharp knife we would extricate them from their parent plant and drop them into the can. There seemed no end to these little guys and many a meal was made complete. In the fall, the plants would go to seed and in the process, drop into the ditches when along with the arrival of water would be carried off to a new home where they would begin the process over again. It still kills me to have to spend two dollars a pound in the store for what once could be had for free.

Chokecherries were another free for the taking fruit that seemed best located up near the Oakley back hills. Although the taste was more on the bitter side, when saddled with lots of sugar, it made a rather tasty concoction which went best on pancakes or waffles. There would have to be a label on those plants now as I wouldn't know a choke cherry from a cough berry. Once again, where are our grandmothers when we need them to show us the way?

Potato Harvest

Probably no other event was anticipated more than the yearly bout with the spud. Fortunately there were no labor unions or 'right" groups to meddle into that glorious event. As potatoes were a major crop for Burley, some body had to get them out of the ground and into the stomachs of our American people. School would close for a period of roughly two weeks and most all would find jobs working for our friends in the fields. We would meet at an appointed spot like the old Burley High School where farmers would show up and select the gatherers. It was a major social event for all and once selected, we would be carted off to the hinterlands to eventually arrive to our new battleground. There was the old Farmall or John Deere (known lovingly as the Poppin Johnny) with a weird contraption which was pulled from behind that awakened the little guys from their summer beds and deposited them on top of the freshly turned soil with their little eyes wide open. Southern Idaho owned some of the best soil, as it was volcanic and sandy in nature, which afforded a wonderful bedtime for the little tubers. The days were spent 'picking potatoes' and either placing them in baskets and into a sack or if you were really a 'man' you wore a harness and while piled with a ton of bags pulled behind you, crawled forward dragging the sack between your legs as you deposited them one spud after another. When full, you unhooked it and after stacking it upright, started over again and again and again.... There was sort of a code of honor and it was not fair to cheat on the exact count or fill of the sacks. As I remember, it worked well. Lunchtime was fun as we delved into our sack lunch which our dear moms made that morning and replaced the empty in our stomachs. I don't recall the outdoor toilet issue. As we were a co-ed group I suspect in hindsight it was not easy being a girl but I never heard any issues about it. It was only until later years did this become an issue (and rightly so.) For entertainment, we played Spud Gladiators. The meanest and biggest potato was selected and we took turns slamming them into our opponents tightly holding hands until one of the poor devils was reduced to mush. There sure were lots of dead bodies lying about when the farmer would enter the scene. Thankful for us, most farmers were of very good nature...We had the most glorious views of Mount Harrison to the south and a good buddy of mine named John Davis was oft heard saying 'boy doesn't Mount Harrison look good!' As with all things good, the weeks would end and back to school we would go. One of first orders of school business was to tabulate those who made the most money.. It was always a fun time and I have no recollections of anyone's self esteem being permanently deranged and later turning into a mass murderer. Of course in those days, things like that were not in vogue. Social engineering would come much later.

When I recall my favorite farmer list, it would have to be topped by Morris Baker who let me work for him on many occasions. What a lovely man. Thank you Morris Baker. And thank you for letting me watch a baby horse being born with all the

visual effects necessary for that sort of thrill.

Number Please

Cell phones hadn't arrived on the scene at that time and all we had was a boring black heavy object called a telephone. Where was the dial? Where was the dial tone? Silly you, all you had to do then was to take the phone from the receiver (that was what it was called) and a pretty girl on the other end would ask you "number please". What could be easier. We didn't have those awful menus of today to wade through. Usually that pretty girl was Peggy Serpa and I recall on more than one occasion of visiting for a few minutes before I gave her the number . Peggy later gave up the phone for Garth Payne which was a better deal for Peggy than listening to me.

Check Your Oil, sir?

When was the last time that someone at a no-service station asked you that? Just west of the ole Haight motors was one of the best gas stations ever. Scotty and son Sammy was always there to service your entire automobile. They had the Texaco gas and service station and you were barely able to get out from behind the wheel before Sammy had his whisk broom doing your floors. Out would come the mats and whisk, whisk, and whisk. Next would come the lift up the hood and the "check thing" (which we seldom do for ourselves today). First came the dip-stick thing (that's the long metal rod reaching into the bottom of the oil pan. Batteries were next and topped off with solution as needed. Not to forget the water in the radiator! Oh and a quick check of the fan belt, water leaks, and any thing that was about to fail on your next trip to Raft River. Lastly after spending a whopping couple

of dollars for gasoline, came the bugs and stuff on the windshield.

Of course the windshields were cleaned inside as well as outside.

The tire pressure was always checked for compliance. On days

when it was time for a lube and oil change, we would take the

auto in for a special service. They even had real repair facilities

with someone who could work wrenches. Often Sammy would

come to the house and pick up the car and then when the auto

was finished, he would return with to out house with a ready to

go car. (Oh and what's with this Raft River thing? Did they really

do that then?)

Kimberley

Who could ever forget the home of my first pizza. When this strange pie made out of tomato sauce, tons of cheese, and pepperoni arrived on the scene, it seemed that Kimberley was the only source. So off to Kimberley we went and strangely I can still taste that wonderful flavor of a dish that would take the country by storm.

Y-Dell Ballroom

And what could be more saucier than those great parties and events at the Y-Dell. Many famous bands would play there but usually only small town stuff. Everyone from all parts of our county would be there from outlying ranches to office buildings. Good dancing, and I believe that there may have been some booze on the premises. I seem to run into the Declo Dewey's every time and they were so friendly. Do you remember the revolving mirrored globe? I do..

Odd Summer Jobs

Most of my friends had summer jobs. It was merely a thing that we did and looked forward to doing it. Perhaps the leader of all summer jobs was the lawn mowing thing. Clipping was an additional charge made over and above the mowing and when all was done, that $2.oo looked pretty good. Of course if you ran over some rose bushes and cut into the sod too deep, you could expect a lashing from the lady of the house. (It was the ladies that usually did the negotiating and hiring) My toughest but most lovable was Mrs. Deardorf whose husband Harold owned the local Rexall Drug Store.

Snow shoveling was a drag and I chose not to discuss it. Then in order was the newspaper delivery system. The king of the routes were the Salt Lake Tribune followed closely by the Twin

Falls Times . Well Carl and Marvin Wrigley already had the Tribune tied up so that left only the Times News. Choice of the routes were mainly whatever was available and my route was north of the railroad tracks. Every day was the routine of picking up the papers in front of the National Hotel and then later a local service station. Then followed the folding process which for me was slightly easier as the paper was much thinner than the Tribune (a plus for the Times). Either making them resemble a flat square like in a flat flying square saucer or the ole roll and rubber band technique. These were then placed into the sacred bicycle basket mounted on the front handle bars or over the rear fender. Then we launched and began the game of target hitting. Yes, many missiles landed on the roof or in the bushes but good delivery boys never let that happen (and there were good delivery girls, Corinne…) . The two toughest times were the times when rain decided to make life difficult with the then unpaved roads. Rubber tires and mud didn't mix then as well as now. An when all else failed, there was always 'mom'. The other difficult times was 'collection time'. Some of my clients were scary to me at the time and the insides of their homes were dark and spooky. But they always were good folks and I learned much about work then along with making some money. About the only other challenge were the dogs whom we feared. It was said that a mean dog could tear off a leg in one bite. Your defense was to put your feet up on the handle bars and coast. However, this created a new problem of locomotion as bicycle speed was in direct proportion to pedaling effort. You knew that you were in trouble if the dog attack persisted for very long. At some point you had to abort the defense and hope that your leg was still attached to resume pedaling. As with so many 'what ifs' ,none of these bad results ever occurred. Oh and quick thanks to my friend Harvey Krieger who was always there to substitute for me when I came down ill or something like ill...

Realizing that after school sports was not going to happen, I resolved to get a job after school. As I was a seasoned bag boy having launched my career at a Piggly Wiggly store in Hereford Texas earlier, I found work at Jay's Fine Foods which was owned and very carefully presided over by Jay Schofield with his faithful manager John Thompson. I enjoyed this work and soon became attached to many of the Burley folks with whom I would become good friends and acquaintances for most of my remaining Burley years. I graduated to become the 'home delivery specialist' and drove the red Dodge pickup daily taking food goods to our local citizens. Boy it just didn't get better. I worked for Jay for some time and even moved to his new location on Overland. Magna Haxby, you were a good lady and friend and I enjoyed working with you. You see, Magna was Jay's major front 'register specialist'. Some of the best times was when Jay would cross the street for a coffee break (I doubt if it was really coffee as Jay was a very good Mormon.) But during those moments, it was time to grab a goody and sneak off for my own coffee break. One of the gourmet snacks was occasional sliced ham from Russ the 'meat specialist' and along with some sneaky cheese in our cracker stash located in the basement we enjoyed the high life. Russ was a great friend and a good butcher even it he referred to Bryce Gochnour as 'shoes' which apparently was related to his two big feet. Among the other unpreventable events were the occasional dropping and

subsequent breakage of those very tasty water melons. Pity....

I became a "farm worker specialist' and worked for several

notable farmers at various seasons. Sam and Cordelia Shaw lived

west of town and worked very hard on their land. The worst of

the duties was the hoeing of beans which I always felt was way

below me but what the heck, they were the boss's. I remember

that I almost killed Sam accidentally while loading hay off of a

wagon with a Jackson fork. When making the move as Sam took

his position on the haystack, I suddenly and inadvertently tripped

the fork which immediately opened up like the land version of

'Jaws' and Sam dived through the depths of hay while I made

a silent request of God to spare me first and then spare Sam.

Well, all went well and I made it through the dress down so well

deserved. They served the best lunches though which made all

work worth while.

Seth Corliss lived on the north side and I worked for him a

spell. Seems a major dance came along and I didn't have a date.

Well why not try some night time plowing. It was a great night on those north side farms running a tractor by headlights and plowing. Boy did I get even with all those poor girls that didn't get the chance to dance with me. (But you know, it may have just been possible that those girls already had dates and may have had a better time). My only major damage which I never owned up was the time I was driving Seth's truck which had those side boards in the down position. It was feed the sheep time and I did just that and drove away. Feeling a sharp 'thump', I jumped out of the truck only to see a dying sheep which never had a chance with me out there. When Seth later arrived and saw the poor lamb, my response was no response. After all, a lie is one thing but if one doesn't say anything, maybe it is not a lie. "Seth I am sorry and you can take it out of my next check ok?" There was one more highlight with Seth Corliss and that was mowing hay with a horse propelled mower. Man that horse knew the game and all one had to do was just hang onto the reins and look important. When nearing the end of the row, the horse would make the left turn and start a new row. I have never experienced anything like that and will never forget it. I guess that could be an early cruise control. Oh I forgot about running through a nest of game birds. I

believe that I did do damage. Sorry birdies..

Water Witching

I believe that his name was Luther Warren. Marilyn and Max Larson along with and Lamar Craner had purchased some land west of Burley and now it was time for water. Who do you call? Mr. Warren came out with his scientific instruments which may have consisted of that old 'y shaped' tree limb and after some careful studying of the land, went right to the spot and sure enough a gusher. I suspect that there must be some sort of law against that today like to save a tree or something. But let me tell you it sure worked then.

Sports (or lack of)

I alluded to my weak sport skills even though I usually gave it my best. I suppose that I should have taken early notice when in the early days of 'choose up sides', I was not always an early choice. Even my good buddy Dee Taylor often overlooked me and picked someone else. But I managed and in spite of modern day social engineering was not adversely effected. Maybe it taught me one of life's strongest meanings. I did participate in kid's knothole baseball league and was only fair. For some reason I had a tough time hitting the ball. I was quite good at playing 'Five Hundred' and 'Knock Out and Roll In'. Basketball was a bit better and I did make a few trips. I remember those early sessions of class when the day was reviewed and the games were announced along with those students who would be excused. Soon, my name started disappearing. Oh well, another of life's lesson. I played for the golf team and tennis team and enjoyed the trips. One major mistake was made with the tennis ladder. It seemed that the time when I finally made the top, I was sent to the bottom to start again. Not realizing that this was good, the brat in me took my tennis ball and went home. Ellis Boden, sorry about that.

J.R.Simplot

From as early as I can remember, this man conjured images of a giant. In many trips to Declo, we would see his place of business and conversation would move to Simplot stories. I recall that he had named a couple of sidings for his two sons, Dick and Don. I thought that quite exciting. Lamar Craner was close to Mr. Simplot so between Lamar and my dad probably, because of "spuds", I became very knowledgeable of the man. My story has it that the eighth grade was enough for 'Jack'. On a couple of occasions, he would send his plane down to Lake Havasu to transport Lamar and Pearl Craner back to Idaho. Well he did well and I know that he had many good feelings about the Burley area and now the Burley International Airport proudly bears his name. As I travel around the Santa Maria valley here in southern Califfornia, I see his name and silently say to myself, "I know that man" (but as with Bill and Harry, he is Mr. Simplot to me..) And what I like so much about him today, is his giant American flag flying over his home in Boise. Right on.......(Sadly I have heard that some neighbors have objected to the flapping noise. Geeze so much for patriotism.. Oh my!)

Winter Time

We made more than the 'best of it' when the snow came as lots of good times were had by all. Do you remember the art of hooky bobbin? Supposedly it was very dangerous but just like the bee-bee gun story, I don't recall anyone dying. Anyway, you had to have some ice on the roads before you could do this. Then you would hide at an intersection for some unsuspecting car to stop. As soon as the car moved forward, you snuck up like the sneak that you were and grabbed hold of the bumpers setting your feet together on the ice and away you would go. Of course in those days, the bumpers were real bumpers and not made out of plastic. A word of caution for those of you who might consider doing this. Avoid the area near the exhaust pipe as it stinks and might even make you ill.

The other major event was those trips out into the countryside on those snowy roads while you sat on your American Racer sled. You could usually get three people who were all bundled in their warmies including their galoshes and sitting in the sled, were pulled by the car in front of you. As you weaved from side to side, the fun was taking on all those drifts that were piled on the sides of the roads. This was the original 'whoosh'.. On occasion, the snow and ice gave way to some gravel and that was a trip. When you become too cold, terrified, or just frazzles, you signaled the car with a hand sign and the car would stop and you could sit in the warm back seat. Of course it was important to not slide under the care as you were stopping as it might damage the American Flyer. Hot chocolate was sure to follow. Here I am sure that the social engineers have stopped this most dangerous event. So what is left? Go out and steal some hub caps.

The Snake (river)

Much of my growing up centered around our river which flowed through our countryside. Exploring was the major event and we would go down on numerous times armed with wooden spears and knives looking for all sorts of big game. One had to watch out for the 'quick sand' or that was what we called it and we were always quick not to step into the mess. Often we would make a small fire and eat our lunch. Actually on one occasion, believe it or not I managed to spear a duck and brought him down. We lunched on that mallard and felt like the big hunters that we weren't. My mom never did approve of the river stuff as she was deadly afraid of it and especially the snakes. Boy that lasted with me for most of my adult life. Thanks mom…It is interesting to look at all those beautiful homes on the river where at one time is was nothing but cattails quick sand, and snakes.

There was Rotary Beach near the base of the present Heyburn bridge and that was our local swimming place. I didn't do well then as now --I was a lousy swimmer. Once more, Rita warned me of the big undertows and huge snakes that resided there. What do you do, you follow mom's advice...

Later I would water ski with Mike Hanzel as my fears seemed to be going away. It was lots of fun jumping (or trying) the jump ramp that someone had placed out in the middle. After getting the air back into your lungs following the usual crash, we simply got up and did it again. Many memories of falling down in the middle and standing up in the middle on a mud pile. I never did encounter those monster undertows.

Enter E.Corinne Terhune

What parent doesn't want a Mozart or a Beethoven for a son. Mine were no different and I never complained as I wanted to take piano lessons. The piano was an old upright with cigarette burns along with some of the ivory missing on the keys. The seat was one of those round and windy ones. My grandpa had found this at the Elks club and so my career was launched. Mrs. Terhune was a feisty little lady but a teacher well respected. For most of my early times, I was in fear of her and did just as she wanted. I took all the way through four or five of the Thompson Red Books and did pretty well. The local recitals were nervously attended but somehow we all made it through with our moms and grand moms watching on with those proud and beaming looks. Many a dark morning was spent practicing for that required 'hour' But the day came when I was no longer afraid of E.Corinne Terhune and one day I decided that I had enough. It was a sad day for all but we move on. But I never forgot her or her son Dr. Charles Terhune who brought me into this world. He was the Doctor of all Doctors. A small tidbit..Those of you who remember our Senator Dworshak for whom one of our schools was named, was supposed to have been a relative of the great compose Dvorak best know by me for his "New World Symphony". They lived on the corner of thirteen street and Conant right close to the Holcombs. Oh, who was this guy 'Conant'? Any takers?s

Those Early Doctors

As mentioned before, we had some of the best doctors in the world. They wore suits, had class, knew medicine, worked very hard, and knew people and how to care for them. For fear of leaving others out I will never -the -less pay my respects to Doctors Kelly, Kircher, Dean, Davis, Annest, and Terhune. This was a time of classy docs who were really 'Jack's of all trades. And do you remember all those house calls with those little black bags? On many occasions when a call was made to Dr. Charles Terhune (his lovely wife Ruth always referred to him as Charles) and at the end a a busy day he would show up to my house and treat whatever little thing was bothering me at the time. It was Doctor Charles Terhune that inspired me to choose my profession. But it was one trip to Sun Valley which having been delayed by an expecting mother to be, made me change my mind and follow the steps of a fine Rupert dentist to make a slight job change. For some reason I liked the hours better. Doctor Dan Slavin was such an inspiration to me. The son of Charles was a friend of mine. Chuck Terhune followed his dad's footsteps and became another fine physician in the state of Washington. We were both attending Northwestern University together. Doctor James Kircher was on the scene later and I ran into him on one of my recent visits to Burley. I am glad that they did not see the advent of the new medicine and the HMO movement but I suspect that they would have carried on as they did and not get deeply involved in them. Some people just don't sell out.

The Night Time Scene

The best of times was the evening drags on our main streets

and especially on the Friday and Saturday nights. For one dollar

of regular gas, you could spend all night doing the same thing of

up and back and around the turn and then up and back again.

Windows were rolled down and you hailed everyone. Man were

we bad. Somewhere along the way, you had to stop for a coke and

burger. Price's Drive-In (Hap...), which was squeezed in between

where a bank and another new store presently is located, had the

best of all barbeques. I am salivating as I write this. For about a

buck you could eat like a king or queen. About the worst drug

that entered the scene was beer and I can't recall it a problem.

Violence was absent and no one got out of line. Our cars were our persona and amounted to everything important. The girls loved it and what else could there have been. We had everything.

Of course what would life have been without those pits of passion. We were in heaven with the Alfresco over the river. Who cared about the movie for after all how could you see it with the windows all fogged over? That was love (or was it lust?) at it's best .And oh we were so sneaky as we smuggled friends into the place by hiding them in the trunks of our cars. I'll bet they never suspected. Wrong! America -lost so much with the disappearance of the drive-in movies. Goshes, now days our kids simply check in and out motels and stuff. Did I tell you that I walked fifteen miles through the snow to go to school?

The Trains

Well we were not on the main line so our train traffic was somewhat limited. We had a couple of local freight trains to carry our potatoes to market and then there was the 'Galloping Goose' which looked a lot like a small trolley car as it loped up and down the tracks. The best times were placing coins on the tracks of an oncoming train so as to flatten the coin for purposes which I have never been sure. There was one thing that you didn't do and that was never place your tongue on a very very cold track. Rumor had it, as I never tried this stunt, your tongue would be glued on as if stuck with Crazy Glue and you would die under the wheels of that fast freight. And of course you should never get too close to a passing train because my mom said that you would be instantly sucked into the train and ground to smithereens. I wonder if that happened to nearby dogs and cats? I remember that when the circus came to town, they would often arrive by train and you could hear the sounds late in the night as they off loaded. I loved the sound of the trains going into reverse and then forward with the sounds of the steam and metal. On those very cold Idaho winter nights the sound of the whistle sounded so eerie as it tried to cut through the barrier of cold.

Later I would catch the Portland Rose for my trips to Chicago for school. The big city where the terminal was located was Minidoka Idaho population of "not much". One would arrive there late in the night and wait and wait watching the old Regulator clock tick back and forth. Snacks, there were none with only wooden benches to sit on. When the time came for the arrival and stop of the train, the railroad man would take a flare and walk up the track a bit, find a good place, and stick it into the nearest railroad tie at the same time igniting the red flares. Steven Spielberg eat your heart out. This was like Twilight Zone and I was about to enter it. The train always stopped but never in the right place. We would walk for many a car length and then finally get aboard on any old car walking the rest of the way to our assigned seating in the dark amidst all the snoring. I met a man who had lived in Minidoka. It seems that his dad saw him throwing rocks down into the green stuff at the bottom of his local outhouse. Well guess who had to crawl down and remove all those rocks? Child protective services where are you when we need you? Gosh, I wouldn't give up those days for all the spud cellars in Acequia.

The Bullies

Thanks that our social engineers have outlawed bullies but where were they when I needed them? For some unknown reason I acquired a couple of bullies somewhere in my early teens. I don't have any clue as to their origin but they were always there and off I would go (like in run).Somehow I always found a safe haven or else I might not be here at this moment. I remember their names but I will keep it my little secret. Well I have often wondered as to what ever happened to them. They should know by now that I 'ain't' afraid of them so let 'em' come. I do know that they probably went to the Miller school and perhaps for that reason I never wanted to go to the Miller school. When my folks would want to scare me, all they had to do was to say that "I was going to be sent to the Miller school". As a side note to those social engineers, it

apparently didn't do me any harm as I grew up anyway…

<u>My Heroes Role Models, and Friends</u>

For me the best part of putting together this little book was the chance to say thanks and a hello and maybe in time a good-bye to some of my favorite people. These people shaped my life in ways which may be unknown to myself and them. I fear that I have too many and yet I also fear that some will be left out. As I will be fine-tuning this tome up to the last minute, hopefully I will achieve my goal. I will mention them in no particular order as they all are special to me in one way or the other. Gosh where to start?

Rita and George Carmody, Wanda and Hal Jolley, Lamar and Pearl Craner, Ella and Bob Pence, Bill Roper, Jim Roper, Harold and Mrs.Deardorf, Jay Schofield, Earl Carlson, Ms. Hagar,Morris Baker,Seth Corless, Sam and Cordelia Shaw, Charles and Ruth Terhune, J.R Simplot, ,

And names that just illicit good memories

These people were simply people that I knew and admired very much in many strange ways. Again I apologize for missing any one or any typo's. Jim Henderson, Bish and Judy Hanzel, Jim Hanzel sr, the Ehlers, the Johnsons and their laundry, Ione and Roma Rambo, Harvey and Maxine Rogers, Holcombs and Smedleys, Loren and Mrs.Lewis, T.Bailey and Irene Lee, Mary Scott, Newell and Miriam Nelson, Frank and Beth Kerns, Russell Shockey, Bill Beck, fire chief Otis Williams amd Bish, Martin Crab, Frank and Betsy Spencer, Arlen and Erleen Taylor, Oberholtzers, Bernice and Joe Olenslagher, the Toolsons, all the Klinks, Fred and Eveline Judevine, Fred and LaVonda Thompson,Mitchells, all those lady bridge players that have escaped my memory,Truman and Liz Bradley, Hoag's, Dominga Obermiller,Sheriff Saul Clarke, policeman Buck Talbot,Harvey Steele, Mrs.Mahoney, Mrs. Hardy (Codingham), Tom Gruel, Clyde and Bertha Gochnour, Cora and Johnny Brooks, Brian and Mrs.Cazier, Fred and Bea Allen, Palmer and Keele Saterstrom, Earl McCaslins, Garrards , Scotty and Sammy Henderson, Kent Lyons,John Thompson, Bill Parsons, Odel Black and Buddy Haight, Buck Stanley, Doctor Wes and Estelle Davis, all the Kuneaus, Senator Dworshak, the Hills, the Taylors, Lois and Irvine Dewey, Retta Payne, Garth and Peggy Payne,the Serpas, the Barlows, Mrs. Burton,the Hills,the Hobsons,John and Jack Snow,Searle and Amelia Powers, Jensens, Rich's, the Blaine Curtis's, Orland Bateman, Al Seed, George Stedman, Rulon and Rusty Stoker (now Mrs. Wally Brown), Wally Brown, Frank and Betsy Spenser, Laidlaws, Carriers, Altha and Iriel Gudmensons, Judge Henry Tucker, the Irv Harris's, McGonigal, Harvey and Maxine Rogers, the Johnsons, the Olenslagers, Frank and Beth Kearns, Harvey and Maxine Rogers, Golden Woods, Wes Bell, Tom and Sadie Church, all those Morgan's, and on and on....

And names of places and businesses

The Mayfair Shop, Roper's Clothing Store, The Burley Drug Store, Jay's Fine Foods, Morgan Hardware Sam and Scotty Henderson's Texaco , Spencer's Office Supply ,Klink's Floral, Harris's Theaters, Rambo's Firestone, Schollar's Jewelry,, Smootch Meacham, Mr. McCormick, Prices Drive-In and Price's Restaurant, the Burley Herald Bulletin, Simplot's, the Reminder, KBIO, Haight Motors, Lee Rooms(never did ok?), Minnies in Declo, Lynch Oil, Van Englands, Penneys, Shelby's Market, Craner Produce, Brooks Produce, Nelson Café, and of course the Oregon Trail Café, Wayne Long Construction, Kiddyville, Harpster's Bakery, McCaslin Lumber, the Burley Stock Yards,A & W Root Beer, Burley Laundry, Fred Sherod's Photography, Millikin's Music, Ike Lee's Furniture Store, Y-Dell Ballroom, Sprague's Pool Room, Baker

Motors, Studebaker Motors,Fronk Motors, Haight Motors, Snyder Furniture, Fulllmers,Declo Drug,Kings and Woolworths, the Herman Kings, Pixtons, Kent Lyons, Don Grayot, National Hotel, the Rainbow. Garrards, the Mayfair, Hanzel Motors, 610 Club, Oregon Trail Cafe

Theater time

Our choices were really only two for any serious theater time. Thank you Irv Harris. There was the Burley theater for the real serious movies and then there was a slightly run down Orphuem theater which is the place that most of us spent our good flick time. Saturdays were the major even and waiting in the line was worth it. Where else could you spend a dime to get into the theater and see not only the main feature but a comedy, a cartoon, some news, and the big event or often a double feature. You had to go regularly in order to catch up on all the chapters ten or was it fifteen of the last week's serial. The good guy or the pretty girl was always left in a lurch and was sure to die-until of course next week. Relief, they were spared but dang if they didn't get themselves into another serious predicament. Popcorn was a deal as it was always freshly popped and better only a dime. We grew up on Roy, Gene, Johnny Mack Brown, Gabby Hayes, Charles Starett, Red Ryder, Froggy, and the Sons of the Pioneers, the Three Stooges, Edgar Kennedy, and course Laurel and Hardy. You know they never said the 'f word' in those movies. Yes there sure was lots of shooting then but you know the blood was minimal and besides the good guy always won. Indiscriminant sex scenes were absent and besides we didn't really care about all that cleavage then. (Boy did that change later down the road.) There was always a good supply of chewing gum (under the seat in front of you of course.)

The Burley theater had those loges where you could take your girl and seem important. I always looked forward to sitting there so that you could wave to all your friends down below I do remember that on many occasions there might be a polio or some other presentation and then the lights would be turned up and a bottle for donations passed. That was a nice thing to do, eh? Of course by this time the tickets had gone up to thirty-five cents. But boy we didn't let that slow us down…Remember when the film would sometimes start to curl and then burn and then the

show would stop for a momentary fix. Another life lesson.

Southwest school

Life growing up in Burley would be incomplete without a trip to Southwest school. So many memories and where to begin. Well, I will begin trying to recall all those great teachers that put up with this show off guy. It all started with Mrs. Beach first grade, Mrs. Hardy(Condinham)second grade, Mrs. Moss third grade, blank fourth grade but remember she was a pretty red head lady (Garner ?),Mrs. Browning fourth grade, Mrs. Mahoney (a very pretty lady), and sixth grade was Harvey Steele and Ellis Boden. Not bad eh? Memories of learning the alphabet in Mrs. Beach's class followed by listening to "Peter and the Wolf" in Mrs. Hardy's class. And to this day every time I hear it, I return to that second grade class room. Some major blanks about major events until my most famous event in the fifth grade when after eating way too many chocolate chip cookies, I decided that it was time to ask Mrs. Mahoney if I may leave the room. Well you guess it, too late for me as I did a number all over the pretty lady. The good news was that as I sat in the car about to be taken home, all my class mates thanked me for letting the entire class leave early. What you gonna do?

We would all march down to the auditorium for occasional group singing. My favorite song and still is today was "the Church in the Wildwood". It was found on some page in that little brown covered book. That same auditorium was a scene of many a play which did play a small part of bringing out my theatrical genius. Oh to just have Joyce Gochnour as my leading lady. Recesses were never excesses. Lots of heavy duty games, sports, and yes we even climbed on the monkey bars. Marbles were a favorite and one of the games was to throw the marble up the water pipe and when it came down, if it was in spanning distance to another's cat-eye, it was yours. Of course the monster of all marbles had to be the 'steelies' which were nothing more than big ball bearings. Look out if one's turn was the 'dropsies'. You could imitate the dropping

of an atom bomb on those little marbles. Kaboomm!

The ditch that bordered our playground was a yearly source of

fun and to my knowledge no one ever drowned. I do remember

Robert Jamison did swim through the culvert located under

road. Of course we were to stay away from it when it was flowing

and there were school guards wearing silly white harnesses to

insure that we never broke the law.. These were the same cops

that made sure you didn't skip any steps when going back into

school. Boy if you were ever caught skipping then it was back to

the bottom of the steps for you. I wonder just how many future

criminals got their start here. Of course in the winter we could

play varieties of catch me if you can and the ditch cops could cop

somewhere else. One of the great games was 'boys chase girls' I

am not sure the real reason for that early hormonal venting, but

is was not complicated, your weren't placed under house arrest,

your name never found the local paper, and not one was ever

hurt. Boy I would not want to do that today (especially at the ripe

age of sixty-six.)

The school nurse used some sort of magic orange wax for kids with toothaches. There must have been plenty of toothaches because lots of wax was used.

On one day I emptied the school. It really was an innocent mistake as I had gone into the basement for something and in looking for a light switch, I let go the switch for the fire alarm. No biggie,eh?

The country kids had to take the bus which always arrived later. Of course when it began the snowy season, it was all up for grabs. I do remember that I never did like those awful brown stockings that all the farm girls would wear to school. Boy, shallow me. They must have had fun riding those neat buses all the time.

I only played hooky once (I think) and I remember hiding in the top of a haystack across where the Davis's and Scofield's lived along with another criminal friend of mine until we saw the school buses return. Then we knew it was alright to head for home. Surely my mom overlooked this one...

Harvey Steele was one of our principals and a very nice man with only one problem. When he would say "everbody do this or

Robert Bailey Lee Carmody

that", it would come out sounding like he was saying "everybaudy" with an accent on the baudy. This isn't nearly as funny as it was in those days when he said it. But we sure did laugh alot.l

Junior and Senior High School

The big jump was ok with no major crises except the girls got better looking and had suddenly done some blossoming over the summer vacation. It looked good. All the classes were good and in particular my eighth grade teacher Mrs. Hagar. She was the queen of English teachers and what with all the diagramming of sentence's and memorizing bits and pieces of literature, I learned much. Sadly I never thanked her for the gift. To this very day I still remember her rules and often shudder when our famous personalities posing as journalists and communicators talk about "Bill and me" or "me and Bill went to town. Do you still remember "is,am,be,are,was,were,been?" Well I do and it still stands for the conjugation of "to be ". Thank you Mrs. Hagar somewhere up there in Albion.

One of the best duties was to work on the staff of the Bur Hur. (Where did they get that name?) The best part was to be officially excused and then off to the Oregon Trail Cafe for coffee and sweets. We had our own private table in the back of the place which was always reserved for us and made journaling so much better. It was a tough assignment but as it has been said so many times before, "someone had to do it."

I must thank Mrs. Bly for her patience with me in our typing class. Had it not been for her, this entire piece would have been scribbled out in long hand (but using that Palmer Method that we learned somewhere at the Southwest.)

Remember the 'Bad Girls from Paul and Acequia'? I know that it does sound like a B movie out of Hollywood but is was our own little B movie. It seemed that they would descend on our ladies with surprise and do battle. The Acequia gals were purported to be the badest of the bad but rumor held that our gals held their own. If the ladies from Acequia were the toughies, the girls from Paul were more on the wild side. Not to mentioned a few names out of respect, I have it from good sources that they always lived up to their reputation. Go Paul.

The man for all seasons has to be my good friend and motivator for my life Mr. Earl Carlson known as "Curly" to all of us smart alecs. This man took charge and ran a good ship and certainly had my respect. He was always present and seldom took any (you fill in the blanks). I will always remember a time when we were filling out our class schedules. He had come into the room and when he looked over mine, he made a most public comment about what a great schedule I had set out to achieve. He constantly nudged me forward. This was somewhere in early seventh or eight grade. He maintained order in those days and I would imagine that even in today's chaotic school environment when anything goes, he would still find a way to maintain that same order. Even though I said that he was a good friend, he did kick my out of school once for wearing short pants to a school assembly. I was to be the master of ceremonies. How could he do that? Well I learned a bit about that and soon put my act into better order. Social engineers take note! I visited Earl and his wife a while ago at their home and was like old times as we reminisced about those great days. Gosh I liked that guy. Dang Mr. Carlson (Earl to many) died late 2003 at around ninety years old. Good by my friend.

Tommy Gruel introduced me to public speaking and one day asked if I would like to participate in some declamation contests. Memorizing speeches seem to come easy and we would present our material to the various service clubs for practice before we traveled to our anointed schools to compete. Needless to say, we all did well and brought home some honors for BHS and for ourselves. This launched me on to better things as years later I took a Toastmaster course and to this day relish the opportunity to stand in front of an audience. I must give you, Tommy Gruel all of the credit.

One cannot forget Rulon Budge and the his Burley Bobcats. He coached some winning teams and I remember those days the man with the magic hand Jack Clark. Along with Jay Jones, Max Larsen, Harold Loveless, the Smith Brothers, Marvin Miller, and others that have momentarily escaped me, they represented Burley very well. Remember the competition between Burley and Rupert? Rupert's Abby Ureugin was their Jack Clark. Two very tough ball teams!

Funny story about labeling. There was this one girl from 'across the tracks'. Rumor had it that she might have a naughty side and sure enough I found all the right evidence that made a lady a soiled dove. For you see she wore pierced ear rings and walked around in ballet slippers. Well you knew immediately what that stood for. I would hope some day to find her and just tell her how badly I felt for those dumb feelings. I really felt stupid when years later my sixty-ish mother in law of very Christian upbringing decided that the time had come for her to pierce her ears. Gad, what had she become?

I must explain the 'across the tracks' thing as I don't want it to come off badly. In the early days most towns had an 'across the tracks'. The origin of that term recently came to light while reading a Stephan Ambrose book about the railroads. For you see all the dirty smoke from those passing trains always drifted to one side or the other. Many times the homes and buildings on the "wrong side' become covered with soot and ash. So it often became the place not to be if you were worried about only your real estate. Well I can tell you that Burley was different for we didn't have a 'wrong side of the tracks' but rather many numbers of very fine people who later become my good friends. And remember, that was the scene of my paper route. It would have been better stated then as the north or south side of the tracks.

Time to move on to some less pleasant memories. About the time I was nearing the ninth grade, I became infatuated with a military school in New Mexico. So as my parents were willing, off I went to New Mexico Military Institute at Roswell, New Mexico. To make it short, I did very well; but, I wanted to return to my Burley High School days. Well the return turned out to be somewhat of a surprise as many of my old acquaintances were harboring some sort of resentment and my early re-entering had a few cloudy moments. I remember a time when I ended up outside on the football field ready for a major event. It involved this pretty lady, Brenda Buttars. (Gad she was cute and her sister Diana was likewise.) We had been dancing at one of those great after game dances. Little did I know she was 'Bobby's girl' and that just didn't fly. Well as things began to get thicker and I was seeing some of my old "friends" taking an opposite side and soon we were outside on the football field for battle. My confusion was interrupted for the moment when Earl Carlson arrived on the scene and in good fashion the event was cancelled. This bothered me for some time but eventually like all things I got through it. Time heals, eh? I never returned later with my pistol or pipe bomb to seek revenge. Boy how things have changed?

This brings me to my old side kick Dee Taylor. We lived just down the alley between the Fronks and Mrs. Kunneau and became friends early. If we weren't playing superman with towels safety pinned around our necks or running through the sprinklers, we were getting into some sort of trouble. It could have been molesting Mrs. Kuneaus fish in her back yard or worse yet throwing dirt on Mrs. Roper's white sheets that were hanging on her back clothesline. Dee's mom was a jewel and was another mother to me. Earleen put up with her naughty boys and of course when all failed then it was time for Arlen. I never knew whether or not Arlen had any shirts as most of the time when I would see him, he was sitting in the chair with a soiled old white tank tee shirt.

On one trip to Sublett reservoir, Dee and I ate the only fish that

Arlen caught for the day. Arlen's favorite word for someone was

"slug". Funny to us and maybe not to you.. Well my mom always

said that I might get into trouble if I hung around with Dee. Well

she was wrong and somehow we made it through.

Bill Roper

My memories of Mr. Bill Roper, he wasn't 'Bill' to me at the time, were that of a Harry Truman look alike. President Truman was a haberdasher and so was Bill Roper. I would have suspected that Mr. Truman, I couldn't have called him 'Harry' at that time, would have run a very similar ship. When you worked at Ropers, you learned how to work. A well respected businessman and a very successful one that taught 'his kids' the art and science of haberdashing was Bill Roper. (Oh, and do your remember that x-ray machine that let you look through a tube and see your toes in their about to be new shoes? That green look was awesome...)My mom had worked for him at some time where she learned her skills which would serve Burley later when she and my dad George Carmody opened the Mayfair women's shoppe. Any way, you were always to look busy when you worked for Ropers. My most favorite and enduring phrase was when you didn't have anything to do, you "sorted socks". You see when customers would come into his store, it was important to have the place looking like a well tuned bee-hive. This instilled confidence into the buying public. "Sorting socks" was nothing more than taking a pile of socks and arranging them into a nice neat pile. That's it! Of course you did that with all the other store items that were for sale. Man, where do you see that today in the modern new way of merchandising? All we see is piles of stuff laying in wild disarray as you walk down the aisles of a Wal-Mart or a K-Mart? Hey WM and KM don't take any offense as it is a different time and we only do what we have been taught. Sadly our 'teachers' and I am not talking about our fine school teachers, are of a different mind set. I continue to use the 'sorting socks' thing with my staff members and always get the same good results. Well Mr. Roper, and may I now call you 'Bill', you taught me a valuable lesson.

Pheasant Hunting

Well we had the pheasant hunting for all seasons. In those early days our fields were abundantly full of that very wily game bird. All one had to do was to get into your car and drive about a couple of miles out of town. The sport was to cruise slowly down the roads until you spotted those long necks sticking above the vegetation. We would then slow down and quietly leave the car. The real challenge was when it came time to get over the fence. One false noisy move and the bird would submerge or fly away. If it didn't fly then it must still be there. We would creep up on the place where we last saw the wily guy (and it had to be a guy because the girls were against the law to kill). Suddenly and unexpected the sky was filled with feathers and a flapping noise that would take at least ten seconds to recover one's wits. If you were lucky and in time you might get a couple of shots away. Boy what a game bird! Oh and do you remember riding on the front fenders through the fields? When you would spot a bird you pounded on the hood which meant 'stop this car now'. As you shouldn't shoot from the car, you jumped off and took your best shot. We did the same thing while standing in the back of a pickup. This was always done best out at the Dewey ranch in Declo with my uncle Hal. He had one problem that should be mentioned here. He had never learned how to tell the guys from the girls (pheasants that is) so on those very rare occasions, he might, and I said "might", bring an occasional hen home. Maybe it was really the fault of his Ithaca featherweight twelve gauge. Yes, that must have been it.

I remember there was a time that the State of Idaho started to crack down on all those Utah pheasant hunters and were beginning to put the screws to them. Well, turn about is fair play so Utah retaliated with ok then we will make it harder for your students to come to Utah for their college. Well, enough said.

That seemed to end the momentary battle and I don't recall it ever coming up again.

The Benevolent Protective Order of Elks

The Elk's club played a very prominent role in early life as many things centered around the club. Perhaps it was in part the fact that my grandpa Bob Pence was a great secretary and earned the nick name of 'Mr. Elks'. The Elks then was a major male hide out from the female set and as one descended into it's smoky depths, many poker games were underway with chips (only?). It was always the same people but for the likes of me the names remain a blank. Maybe Roscoe Rich was there and then again maybe not. As you bellied up to the bar you had to be very careful not to get your foot stuck into one of those shiny brass spittoons. Gad, I cannot believe that they did that back then when they had all those great side walks to spit on. I wonder if they deposited their chewing gum into them also? Don't forget George Steadman. He was always there. The walls were lined with several slot machines and then there were those great war pictures which I mentioned of our young warriors fighting the war. Papa's office was a small room where all the action occurred. He was a major mover and loved his Elks and next to Nanny it was always his best love. Lamar Craner and my dad George Carmody were both 'exalted rulers' and served well. I have pictures of some of those men like Rip Manning and Oscar Lowe. Again great memories rise up to the surface when I think about those great days. Perhaps the New Year's parties were the best. I couldn't wait for the parents to come home with all those goodies so that I could wake the neighborhood on the next morning. Even here today, about the only New Year's party is ,where else ,but at the Elks Club. Just recently they had a Tom and Jerry party here and it recalled those times when the Burley Elks lodge had Tom and Jerrys served during the Christmas holidays. Right on Elks! Do you know that many people have never heard of a Tom and Jerry? I sure hope that the PITA folks don't get word of

Robert Bailey Lee Carmody

this or they might misconstrue it to mean like in the little mouse

person and outlaw this delightful libation.

The Police and Fire Department

Many an adventure was spent visiting the police department and we were locked up in the cells, finger printed, and taken on rides. Once we drove down to the dump across from my old girlfriend and now Wayne Christiansen's lovely wife-Joyce Gochnour. Forgetting Joyce for a moment, we went down the hill into the dump and Buck Talbott did some target shooting with old cans and bottles. The 'cops' were always our friends and there never was a major problem. Of course we seldom had any crime but that was a long time ago. Today in reading the Southern Idaho Press, it looks like there are times when crime is trying to catch up with the national averages. Well ok not really catching up but there seems like there is more now. Buck Talbott, where are you now when we need you?

Have you ever slid down a brass fire house pole? Well sadly not even many of the new fire people have experienced that most exhilarating 'E ticket' ride .Climbing upstairs, you would lean over against the pole, wrap your legs around it, and then launch and downward you flew. Located in the old library building next to the court house, it was a major event to behold. The police and fire people were so 'easy' in those days and I will always have fond memories of my life in the hoosegow and poling into action for the big blaze. Gosh only in Burley!

Burley Drug Store

Harold Deardorf had a great place. Forget all those drugs and stuff, it was that marble fountain with those magical spigots, mirror lined glasses, and secret metal boxes which housed all that ice cream. Root beer floats, phosphates, cherry cokes, grilled ham and cheese sandwiches, and neighbors to visit with. Esther was always somewhere about to keep order and she did it well. Back behind the window was uncle Hal putting together drug orders. I'll bet that there were very few drugs in those days as compared with now so maybe it was easier? Probably only some heart pills, nose pills, stomach pills, and antibiotic pills. That was way before 'the pill' and 'viagra'. There were lots of good free comic book reading which I am sure pleased the staff at old Burley Drug. It seemed that you could buy anything there.

Kid's (Crick) Creek

Every year they would stock that little crick that ran behind the cemetery and later through the golf course. It was opened to us kids and usually there was a prize for the biggest, littlest, ugliest , and whatever. Boy that was fun fishing that little stream as a kid. Do they do that any more? And why not?

Parades

There never seemed an excuse needed for a parade. I do know around the Fourth of July there would be one. And again in the fall near rodeo time we would have one. Every one and every thing participated including the Cassia Country Sheriff's posse to old trucks, new trucks, fire engines, and lots of messy horses. I don't believe that horses were required to wear those bag-diaper things like they do now days. The pre-diaper era made the entire event more real and pleasurable. That road apple production was sort of a back to nature event and it always amazed me as to just how those horses made it work back there. I rode my old blind in one eye 'Socks' with Dickie and Tommy Taylor riding right there behind me. There was always lots of on lookers cheering us on and waving those great American flags. I suppose that now there must be some sort of health department regulation against all

those things. Geez, does Burley even have a Health Department?

Change

My visits to Burley have become fewer and fewer as my clan has diminished it's size. When I do come to visit, I notice the changes that have taken place. On the outside it is not the same Burley of my youth. Many stores are gone or have been name changed. There are too many paper clad windowed empty spaces where once was life. There are different people there where once there were none. The language of the street has more unfamiliar sounds. The town has changed but in reality so have I. It is the nature of life to change or else we would never have new crops or new roses on the vine. A town can change it's outside appearances but it's heart and soul will always remain the same. I see good exiting things ahead with the new cultures that bring an injection of new life. I would hope that this small book might introduce my town to the new folks. Perhaps in a small way it might give them a cameo look at what was. It is an inherent part of man that seeks better ways and changes of things overdue for that change. I doubt that Burley will ever be another Los Angeles and thank God for that. I believe that it will always remain as it has been and will continue to be ...My Home Town. rblc

Printed in the United States
26633LVS00004B/481